GREAT WESTERN ALBUM No 2

Only a local freight train, maybe, but look at the magnificent
pre-1914 war finish of Churchward mixed traffic 2-6-0 No 4331

[BR

GREAT WESTERN ALBUM
No 2

R. C. RILEY

LONDON

IAN ALLAN

First published 1970
Second Impression 1971
Third Impression 1974

SBN 7110 0135 9

Published by Ian Allan Ltd, Shepperton, Surrey, and printed in
Great Britain by Crampton & Sons Ltd, Sawston, Cambridge

Introduction

THERE WAS no line quite like the Great Western—the LNWR may have called itself the "Premier Line", but to GW officer, servant, and enthusiast alike there was only one possible contender for that title. Had not *Polar Star* licked the pants off a hopelessly outclassed LNWR machine in 1910? The same thing happened on the LNER with *Pendennis Castle* in 1925 and on the LMSR with *Launceston Castle* the following year. It was a GWR engine, too, the famous *City of Truro* that was said to have attained the first recorded 100 mph on rails. In recent years it has been fashionable to cast doubts on this achievement but not always with a great deal of conviction.

City of Truro itself may still be admired in Swindon Railway Museum. It certainly deserves its place. It was the eighth of ten "City" class engines built in 1903 and when *City of Exeter* emerged from Swindon in May of that year the era of the double-framed express engine was past. There were still some double-framed 4-4-0s to be built. The "Bulldogs" were built over many years up to 1910 and this type had a curious renaissance in 1936 when GWR official publicity tended to describe as new engines the "Earl" 4-4-0s, those fascinating machines to become better known in later years as the "Dukedogs".

There was another significant feature about the "City" 4-4-0s, too, in that they started the naming of GWR engines in series, the general practice until the last GWR type named engine was built in BR days. The famous "Saint" class 4-6-0s, for example, included "Saints", "Courts", and two batches having literary associations, some from Scott's novels and some distinguished Ladies. Someone once remarked that only the Great Western Railway could possibly have classed *Lady Macbeth* as a Saint!

There was nothing ponderous about *City of Truro's* high speed achievement in 1904. It was the GWRs way of showing what it could do if it tried. On this occasion it was demonstrating that it had the edge over its rival, the LSWR, in handling the Ocean Liner traffic between Plymouth and London. One has to admit, though, that without such an incentive the GWR did not always try very hard. There were those who remarked that the initials stood for the "Great Way Round", and this title was not wholly undeserved in the last century. In 1900 the traveller from Paddington reached Exeter via Bristol, Birmingham via Oxford, and South Wales via Bristol or Gloucester. Motive power was well built and adequate; coaches were well built and uncomfortable. There was nothing to be specially proud of in the timetables.

However, a new era was dawning—the old broad gauge mentality was out. Heavy engineering works were in progress to make more direct routes for what are now known as inter-city services. Passenger services were being expanded and improved. Above all there was a new Locomotive Engineer turning out larger engines than ever before. In 1899, remarkable in retrospect, Dean was still building single-wheelers, the elegant but short lived 4-2-2s. Only seven years later Churchward had had sufficient experience of his two and four-cylinder 4-6-0 designs to start construction of these standard engines in quantity. There was some criticism of the high cost of Churchward's express engines compared with those of the LNWR—hence the 1910 locomotive exchange trials by which Churchward proved the quality of his designs and effectively stifled any further criticism. In 1903 the Badminton route to South Wales was opened, followed three years later by the direct route to the west via Castle Cary and in 1910 by the new route to Birmingham via Bicester. The GWR could no longer be described as the Great Way Round, passenger comfort was improving all the time and the new engines were maintaining accelerated schedules on ever increasing train loads.

World War I inevitably proved a setback to the aspirations of the GWR management as indeed it did to every other major railway company. Highly polished brass domes on the engines vanished for ever, so did the lining out, although this was resumed after the war on the largest express engines; the rest remained in unlined green to the end of the GWR. There was a brief resumption of lining out on lesser engines in BR days. Curiously the once familiar chocolate and cream livery had been discontinued as early as 1908, at first replaced by unrelieved brown but altered four years later to crimson lake. Perhaps Churchward, not prepared to cut the cost of his locomotives had to make economies in other ways.

By 1923 when the railway Grouping took place and the Great Western was the only major company to emerge with its title unchanged, the war had been ended long enough for its adverse effects to have been overcome. Back came the chocolate and cream livery, and with it in that same year came *Caerphilly Castle*, the first new express type since *The Great Bear* of 1908. Perhaps the less said about that large machine the better, beyond mentioning that prestige-wise it was Britain's first Pacific locomotive.

So far as the GWR was concerned it was also the last Pacific and it survived Churchward's retirement at the end of 1921 only by a couple of years. The "Castles" were as successful as the "Stars" from which they were derived, and with the two-cylinder "Saints" little less powerful the GWR led the country in the sphere of locomotives at that time.

Always publicity conscious, the GWR heightened its efforts in this direction in the 1920s, now that it had so much more of which to be proud. In 1923 it produced "The 10.30 Limited", the first of a series of books which were excellent value and are still much sought after. Other titles include "Caerphilly Castle" (1924), "Brunel and After" (1925), "The King of Railway Locomotives" (1928), "Cheltenham Flyer" (1934), "Track Topics" (1935), and "Locos of the Royal Road" (1936). In 1911, the first edition of the "GWR Engine Book" was published, there being many subsequent editions. The "GWR Magazine", first pub-

"Star" Class 4-6-0 No 4015 *Knight of St John* hustles the "Cheltenham Flyer" through Burnham, April 25, 1925
[H. G. W. Household

lished in 1888, was aimed as much at the enthusiast as the staff, whose magazine it first set out to be.

The 10.30 "Cornish Riviera Limited" was always a prestige train and much publicised. First introduced in 1904 it was a heavy train all the year round and for many years carried several slip portions so that by the time it reached the South Devon banks its load was reduced to the maximum allowed for one engine and no stop for assistance was required. Original schedule for the non-stop run to Plymouth was 4 hrs 25 mins over the 246½ miles via Bristol. On the opening of the Castle Cary route 20 miles shorter the time was cut by 18 minutes and both "Stars" and "Saints" put up some fine performances on this train. With the advent of the "Kings" in 1927 the four-hour schedule was introduced that was to remain the best steam timing, although "Castles" achieved some faster runs with less heavily loaded Plymouth Ocean Liner expresses.

It was "Castles" too that put up some lively performances on the equally well publicised "Cheltenham Flyer" that for many years was claimed to be the fastest train in the world. Perhaps the GWR was a little sensitive about the Cheltenham service for at one time it was possible to do the journey from London more quickly out of Waterloo, changing into the MSWJ northbound express at Andover Junction! It must have given some small comfort to the minor company, construction of which had been opposed and hindered in every way by the GWR. The "Cheltenham Flyer" was an existing train from Cheltenham, via Gloucester, which from 1923 was accelerated to cover the 77¼ miles from Swindon and Paddington in 75 minutes, an average speed of 61·8 mph. *Saint Bartholomew* made a spirited run on the first trip, and "Saints" and "Stars" were the regular performers until 1929 when a further five minutes was clipped from the schedule. Two years later the Canadian Pacific Railway introduced a schedule that gave an average speed of

The distinctive pagoda like shelter used on halt platforms. on the branch to Bala

Teigl Halt was attractively situated near Blaenau Festiniog
[*R. C. Riley*

7

The GWR was the first railway company to use motor 'buses. Here is an AEC, No 248 in the 'bus fleet list, on the Stroud-Painswick Road Motor service, November 20, 1924
[*H. G. W. Household*

86·9 mph. The GWRs answer was to cut the schedule to 67 minutes, an average of 69·2 mph, so regaining the high speed laurels, *Launceston Castle* cutting this by more than seven minutes on the first day! In 1932 the schedule improved to 65 minutes or an average of 71·3 mph to give a more positive lead. That this was easily maintained had already been proved when *Tregenna Castle* improved on the 67-minute schedule by more than 10 minutes, an average speed of 81·6 mph and no higher speed than 92 mph.

Although the first stretch of the GWR, 22½ miles between Paddington and Maidenhead, was not opened until 1838, its Act had been authorised three years earlier, in 1835. Hence the GWR chose to celebrate its Centenary in 1935 and apart from the introduction of luxurious new coaches, an example of which is preserved by the Dowty RPS at Ashchurch, it introduced a new high speed train, "The Bristolian", which was usually "Castle"-hauled and ran both ways between London and Bristol, 118 miles in 105 minutes, averaging 71·6 mph. This achievement was overshadowed in the same year by the LNER "Silver Jubilee" which averaged 70 mph on a four-hour run between London and Newcastle with an intermediate stop at Darlington. Two years later the

LNER "Coronation" covered the 188¼ miles from London to York in 157 minutes, its average speed of 71·9 mph just beating the "Cheltenham Flyer" but over a much greater distance, going on to reach Edinburgh in six hours from London. The outbreak of war in 1939 brought an end to all high speed trains and the "Cheltenham Flyer" was never restored afterwards, although "The Bristolian" did eventually re-appear and in the latter years of steam haulage had the schedule cut to 100 minutes, an average of 72·3 mph.

Even if it had dropped to second place in the high speed league, the GWR could still look back on the achievements of the years prior to the war with considerable satisfaction. Many of its major stations, including Paddington, had been rebuilt and resignalled The old dark main line stations with their heavy overall roofs were almost a thing of the past. There were still some stations that could have done with improvement, notably the austere wooden buildings of Oxford and Banbury, while at the other end of the scale there were some older buildings of special architectural significance, notably Bristol Temple Meads and Shrewsbury. For other than important stations corrugated iron was much fancied by GWR station builders between the wars. While the pagoda-like structure that provided a degree of shelter at railmotor halts was quite acceptable, the effect of a preponderance of this building medium was less happy. A dreadful example was Oldfield Park, built to serve the needs of a housing estate outside Bath in 1929, its spartan appearance heightened by the pleasing dignity of other stations on the line.

Although just beaten by the LSWR in the introduction of steam railmotors in 1903 as a useful unit for handling branch line and suburban traffic, the GWR was the largest user of these vehicles and of the railmotor trains developed from them. Also in 1903 the GWR had pioneered the use of motor omnibuses, in which it was followed by most major railway companies. The first service was between Helston and The Lizard, but many more services of what the GWR described as "road motors" were later introduced. Indeed, in 1904 the 36 motor buses of the GWR already in service outnumbered those in London at that time! Between 1929 and 1932 the large GWR fleet of 'buses was dispersed and its services taken over by other companies, in most of which the GWR had a substantial interest. An extraordinary development in 1932 was the introduction of an air service between Cardiff and Plymouth, the northern end of the service soon being extended to Birmingham. The aircraft used were appropriately painted chocolate and cream!

Thirty years after its first steam railmotor the GWR put a diesel railcar into traffic and within ten years it built up a fleet of 38 such vehicles. In 1934 some powerful express railcars were introduced between Birmingham and Cardiff. A buffet service was provided and the traffic developed by the railcars soon brought about their replacement by steam trains running on similar fast schedules. One example of this type of vehicle, Railcar No 4, has been preserved by BR and is in the custody of the Great Western Society in Didcot shed. Two of the later cars have also been preserved and one of these is on a branch where such vehicles were regularly used, the Severn Valley line, scene of an ambitious and worthy preservation venture.

GWR enthusiasts have indeed excelled in the field of railway preservation. So many engines and other rolling stock items have been preserved that it is hard to keep track of them all! The Great Western Society for example, has a dozen locomotives, two railcars and 14 coaches preserved at various places. Since preservation is a costly business both in time and money it cannot be too greatly stressed that such activities deserve the support of all Great Western enthusiasts. While there can never be enough members prepared to put in days, weeks, or even months of work on menial tasks such as track relaying, culvert clearing, paint stripping, or

The GWR introduced the popular Camping Coaches in 1931. Coach No 9982 was a 1934 conversion of No 6218, a composite coach of 1884 vintage
[G. H. W. Clifford

While the GWR was conventional in many respects its signals only conformed to the convention of being lower quadrant. Otherwise they varied in design and the down starters at Kingham were of a type intended to ensure ease of visibility where a station awning might otherwise make sighting difficult [*J. P. Wilson*]

renewing the sadly decayed woodwork of an elderly coach deteriorated by years of departmental service, the armchair member prepared to pay an annual or a life subscription also takes part by contributing the necessary funds to keep preservation going. In return members are kept in touch with activities by regular newsletters and magazines, those of the Great Western Society and Severn Valley RPS in particular being excellent productions well illustrated and printed on art paper. Although primarily a commercial venture, the Dart Valley line also has its supporting association, for it relies as much as the other societies on volunteer labour to keep its preservation activities going, and DVRS members are also kept informed of events by regular magazines.

The steam era may be over on the Great Western, and its identity submerged for more than 20 years as part of BR, but nevertheless there remains a great deal to be seen and GWR enthusiasts are fortunate in having an abundance of literature available on the subject. In compiling this second Great Western Album I am grateful to all those photographers and owners of collections, who kindly allowed me to make use of their pictures. As before the experts among the membership of the Historical Model Railway Society gave some worthwhile advice, notably Jack Slinn and Colin Strevens on the subject of rolling stock. An impressive amount of information on a variety of topics is condensed into the GWR Livery Register published by the HMRS, while the 12-volume locomotive history of the Railway Correspondence & Travel Society is equally indispensable as a work of reference. The present publisher's catalogue includes many books on GWR topics including a useful reprint of the standard history by MacDermot, a reprint of a 1904 timetable, also the Company's Rules and Regulations published in the same year. A book that conveys the best word picture of the GWR between the wars, its idiosyncrasies described with an amused but kindly tolerance, is George Behrend's "Gone With Regret", for which I chose the illustrations. Finally I must express my gratitude to all those readers of "Great Western Album" who wrote to the publishers to express their appreciation. If the present volume receives as much support it will not be long before work starts on Great Western Album No 3!

No 4086 *Builth Castle* heads the 1.45pm Paddington-Stourbridge near Reading West Junction in 1945. This engine attained 100mph down Honeybourne bank with the 12.45pm Paddington-Hereford train in 1939, the first recorded GWR "ton" since *City of Truro's* exploit in 1904   [*M. W. Earley*

LEFT: The original 7ft gauge favoured by the GWR made for comfortable travelling but not for easy interchange—trans-shipment of freight traffic was particularly burdensome. A down passenger train approaches Maidenhead at the time of track widening works carried out between 1890 and 1893. The track has already been converted to "mixed" gauge, to allow broad and standard gauge trains over it   [BR

BROAD GAUGE

BELOW: *Dragon* was one of 24 singles built at Swindon in 1880—indeed construction continued until 1888 so the later engines had only four years of life as the last broad gauge lines were converted to standard gauge in 1892   [BR

A down broad-gauge express approaching Bath towards the end, with mixed gauge track in evidence
[LPC

Swindon Junction in mixed gauge days. The up train is a standard gauge train
[Museum of British Transport

Broad gauge tank engines on the dump at Swindon Works after the 1892 gauge conversion   [L&GRP

13

ABOVE: Towards the end of the broad gauge era over 100 engines were built as "Convertibles". Among these were ten 2-4-0 tanks of 1885, five of which were altered to tender engines in broad gauge days. In this condition No 3508 was recorded at Exeter shed. All ten became tender engines on conversion to narrow gauge

[HMRS Collection

THE EARLY SCENE

BELOW: The "3201" Class numbered 25 engines, of which five were built as tender engines, the remainder being converted from broad gauge tanks (3501-10) and narrow gauge tanks (3511-20). No 3202 was one of the original engines but its polished brass dome had been painted by the time this photograph was taken. Several of these engines lasted until the early thirties

[BR

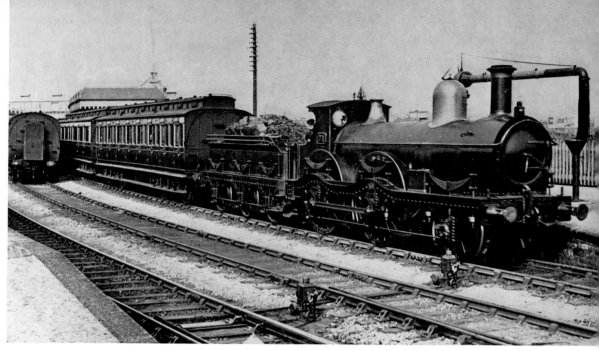

ABOVE: The eight "River" class 2-4-0s of 1895-7 were classed as renewals of old Singles. They were charming little engines, long associated with the London and Bristol divisions. No 71 *Dee* was withdrawn in 1913 but two others survived five years longer　　　　　　　　　　　　　　　　　　　　[BR

The last new 2-4-0s built were the 20 engines of the "3232" class built 1892-3. One survived on the Cambrian section until 1930, but most were broken up in the twenties. No 3239 heads a down express near Iver　　　[C. Laundy/K. H. Leech

ABOVE: Among the most handsome and best known of GWR engines the 80 Dean 7ft 8in 4-2-2s were built in the nineties, the first 30 having started life as 2-2-2s, some in "Convertible" form. Many of them revived the names of early broad gauge engines, *Lord of the Isles* being one well known example. Regrettably they had short lives and all were gone by the end of 1915. No 3037 *Corsair* was recorded at Westbourne Park shed, closed in 1906 when Old Oak Common opened [*LPC*]

DEAN SINGLES

BELOW: No 3053 *Sir Francis Drake* heads an up Bristol express near Iver. Note the 70ft "Concertina" type brake third of 1906 vintage leading. With their recessed doors these coaches had a greater route availability than the better known "Dreadnoughts" introduced in 1904 [*C. Laundy/K. H. Leech*]

ABOVE: As built in the late nineties the famous "Dukes" had straight nameplates along the front of the boiler side. The more familiar curved nameplates were fitted from 1903 onwards and what a glorious sight these engines looked with all the traditional polish prior to World War I. No 3272 *Amyas* was renumbered 3266 in 1912 and survived at Didcot until 1937   [*BR*

DEAN 4-4-0

BELOW: The "3521" class were built as 0-4-2 or 0-4-4 tanks, some as broad gauge "convertibles", but being prone to derailment all were rebuilt as 4-4-0 tender engines, in which form a few survived until the thirties. No 3527 has the magnificent finish of pre-war days   [*BR*

LEFT: The "Metro" tanks were so known because of their long association with through trains to the Metropolitan Railway, for which purpose many were condenser fitted. Over 30 years from 1869 Swindon built 140 of these 2-4-0 tanks and ten of the later engines survived to come into BR hands. No 1464, built in 1882, was recorded at the old shed at Cheltenham about 1910
[A. K. Pope Collection

RIGHT: The "1016" class 0-6-0 saddle tanks were built at Wolverhampton between 1867 and 1871. Most of the 60 engines were rebuilt with Belpaire boilers and pannier tanks from 1911 onwards. No 1033 in the dead end at Cheltenham shed was built in 1867 and lasted over 60 years
[A. K. Pope Collection

BELOW RIGHT: Much later on the scene were the 36xx 2-4-2 tanks, 31 of which were built between 1900 and 1902. This wheel arrangement was not as popular on the GWR as on other lines, notably the LNWR and the GER, and all were withdrawn by 1934 having been replaced by 2-6-2 tanks. In later years some engines had number plates moved to the bunker sides, but most of them remained in similar form to No 3604
[Eric Mason, courtesy A. G. Ellis

EARLY
TANK
ENGINES

BELOW: While Swindon was building 2-4-0 tanks Wolverhampton remained faithful to the 0-4-2 tank type. The "517" class eventually numbered over 150 engines and like the "Metro" tanks there were many variations. Built between 1868 and 1885 the earliest engines originally had saddle tanks. No 541, built in 1869, was among these and was also recorded at Cheltenham
[A. K. Pope Collection

LEFT: First express 4-6-0 was No 100 built in 1902 and named *William Dean* later that year when its namesake retired through ill health and Churchward took over, although he had been Locomotive Engineer in everything but name for some time. No 100 is here heading west out of Dawlish. The nameplate was transferred to the driving splasher in 1906. This engine was never modified to conform with the standard "Saints" and was withdrawn in 1932   [*Chapman & Son*

RIGHT: In later form as a 4-6-0 No 2984 *Guy Mannering* (formerly 184) heads a down express past Old Oak Common East signalbox in 1913. The horse box marshalled after the fourth coach in the middle of the train is a curiosity. Note too the 0-6-0 saddle tank with polished dome leaving the sidings with empty stock for Paddington   [*E. Ashcroft*

CHURCHWARD EXPRESS ENGINES

LEFT: After an era with such lovely engines as the Dean Singles the early Churchward engines were at first criticised for their exposed wheels and general severity of line. No 98, later *Ernest Cunard*, was the true forerunner of the famous "Saint" class and as No 2998 lasted until 1933   [*J. L. Smith Collection*

RIGHT: At the same time as Swindon was building the two-cylinder "Saints" it was also turning out the four-cylinder "Star" class 4-6-0s. In pre-war condition No 4017 *Knight of the Black Eagle* heads an up mail train through St Annes Park, Bristol. Because of its Germanic associations the name was removed in August 1914 and No 4017 became *Knight of Liege*   [*L&GRP*

LEFT: In 1905 Swindon turned out Nos 172-90, of which only 173-8 were built as 4-6-0s, the others running until 1912 as 4-4-2s. In this form No 180 *Coeur de Lion* approaches Teignmouth with the down "Cornish Riviera" in 1908   [*R. Brookman, courtesy K. H. Leech*

CHURCHWARD EXPRESS ENGINES

ABOVE: The "Saints" so named were the 2911-30 batch and with 2931-55 named after Courts formed a standard series of this class with many variations. No 2930 *Saint Vincent* was posed at the head of the 1897 Royal Train in 1910. The one time Queen Victoria's saloon is towards the rear. The brake coaches survived in departmental use until recent years and one is illustrated behind 2-8-0 No 4707 in the first GREAT WESTERN ALBUM   [BR

BELOW: Churchward's 4-6-2 No 111 *The Great Bear* at Paddington in 1910 with a Bristol express. Built in 1908 it was heavier and longer than the SR "Merchant Navy" class and this bulk considerably restricted its activities. Basically an enlarged "Star" 4-6-0 it seems to have been built primarily for reasons of publicity and prestige. Churchward is said to have disliked the engine but it survived until two years after his retirement in 1922   [J. L. Smith Collection

LEFT: Churchward always took a great interest in foreign railway practice and in 1903 he ordered a 4-4-2 similar to the successful compound engines of the Nord Railway of France. In 1916 it was rebuilt with a standard taper boiler and lasted a further ten years. No 102 *La France* stands at Moreton-in-Marsh on a Paddington-Worcester express, August 1923
[*H. G. W. Household*

FRENCH
ATLANTICS

BELOW: In 1905 two more French compounds were ordered, this time of Paris-Orleans Railway design, Nos 103 *President* and 104 *Alliance*. Both eventually carried standard taper boilers and No 103 is seen at Paddington in this form. They were withdrawn in 1927 and 1928 respectively [*BR*

STAR
CLASS
4-6-0

ABOVE: No 4005 *Polar Star* attained a considerable degree of fame in 1910 when it ran exchange trials on the Paddington-Exeter and Euston-Crewe lines with the LNWR 4-6-0 *Worcestershire*. At that time both engines were unsuperheated but *Polar Star* was the more powerful of the two and its superior performance on all counts could have been anticipated. It is here seen at Paddington on the 3.15pm Cheltenham express, May 16, 1925   [*L&GRP*

BELOW: No 4035 *Queen Charlotte* approaches Twyford with a down express consisting largely of early Collett design coaches   [*BR*

ABOVE: No 4045 *Prince John* heads a Birmingham-Paddington express near Harbury tunnel about 1925. The second coach appears to be of Cambrian Railways' origin [*Mensing-Osborne Collection*

BELOW: On less exacting duty *Prince John* approaches Patchway with a Cardiff-Portsmouth train, 1938 [*G. H. Soole*

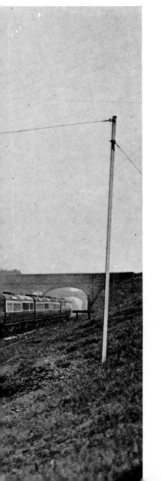

"SAINT" CLASS 4-6-0

ABOVE LEFT: No 2903 *Lady of Lyons* approaching Patchway with the Wood Lane-Whitland milk empties. Note the "Siphon G" bogie van at the head of the train
[*G. H. Soole*

BELOW LEFT: No 2937 *Clevedon Court* stands at the head of an up express at Birmingham Snow Hill, February 20, 1939. This engine was station pilot at Reading one day in 1938 when a "King" working the down "Bristolian" high speed express broke down. Despite several checks *Clevedon Court* improved on the exacting schedule and ran the 82 miles to Bristol at an average speed of 72mph
[*N. Shepherd*

ABOVE: No 2946 *Langford Court* near Patchway with the 11.35 am Carmarthen-Bristol train, March 1937. This was an easy task for the engine but the "Saints" were certainly flyers when the occasion demanded
[*G. H. Soole*

27

ABOVE: No 5010 *Restormel Castle* as built in 1927 with 3,500 gallon tender heads an up Birmingham express near Bentley Heath   [*W. L. Good*

"CASTLE" CLASS 4-6-0

BELOW: No 7013 *Bristol Castle* tackles Campden bank with an up Worcester express, April 6, 1957. This engine was none other than the one time Royal Engine No 4082 *Windsor Castle* of 1924. It was at Swindon Works at the time of the death of HM King George VI and changed identities with the 1948 built No 7013, a change that was to remain permanent   [*C. F. H. Oldham*

ABOVE: Just over the summit of the three mile climb of Hemerdon bank, largely at 1 in 42, No 5098 *Clifford Castle* heads a Plymouth-Liverpool express, July 5, 1955

[*R. C. Riley*

"CASTLE" CLASS 4-6-0

The last ten "Stars" Nos 4063-72 of 1922/3 were rebuilt to "Castle" class in the late thirties as some earlier engines had been. No 5083 *Bath Abbey* heads the 1.0pm West London Sidings-Shrewsbury parcels train near Old Oak Common, October 19, 1957 [*R. C. Riley*

"KING" CLASS 4-6-0

The "Kings" superseded the "Castles" as the GWRs most powerful engines in 1927. All were fitted with double chimneys in BR days and in this condition No 6001 *King Edward VII* heads the 1.10pm Paddington-Birkenhead out of the terminus, April 16, 1957   [*R. C. Riley*

"KING" CLASS 4-6-0

ABOVE: No 6014 *King Henry VII* heads a down Wolverhampton express near Bentley Heath. This engine was subsequently chosen for a misguided experiment in streamlining [*W. L. Good*]

BELOW: No 6026 *King John* in charge of the heavy down "Cornish Riviera Express" near West Drayton in 1936 [*W. H. C. Kelland*]

ABOVE: No 6014 *King Henry VII* with part of its stream-lining in place heads a down express out of Exeter in 1936   [*W. H. C. Kelland*

BELOW: No 6024 *King Edward I* in final form with the later pattern of double chimney steams Londonwards on the up 7.45am Bristol near Chippenham, March 5, 1959   [*K. H. Leech*

ABOVE: The "Halls" were the first mixed traffic 4-6-0s introduced in 1928, based on the rebuilding of No 2925 *Saint Martin* with 6ft wheels. No 4923 *Evenley Hall* heads the 8.45am Plymouth-Manchester express pa t Patchway, in original form with 3,500 gallon tender

[*G. H. Soole*

"HALL" CLASS 4-6-0

BELOW: A Manchester-Plymouth express threads the Shropshire countryside near Church Stretton in charge of No 5905 *Knowsley Hall*   [*Dr Ian C. Allen*

ABOVE: No 4988 *Bulwell Hall* emerges from Holywell Tunnel with a Yeovil-Weymouth stopping train, September 4, 1948
[*Donovan E. H. Box*

RIGHT: No less than 258 "Halls" were built in similar form to *Saint Martin*, which was modified to conform to the standard pattern. Between 1944 and 1950 a further 71 "Modified Halls" were built to Hawksworth's designs. No 6965 *Thirlestaine Hall* of this type heads down Penzance milk empties near Hungerford, July 8, 1956
[*R. C. Riley*

ABOVE: Between 1936 and 1939 Collett built 80 "Granges", similar to the "Halls" but with 5ft 8in wheels. These were most useful and versatile engines. No 6820 *Kingstone Grange* heads the Exeter-Rogerstone coal empties train near Patchway   [*G. H. Soole*

"GRANGE"
CLASS
4-6-o

BELOW: Always popular on Summer Saturday extra trains a Paignton-Wolverhampton train approaches Exeter St Davids in charge of No 6848 *Toddington Grange*, July 19, 1958   [*R. C. Riley*

ABOVE: The 30 "Manors" were a lightweight version of the "Granges", suitable for working on lines where there were restricted axle loadings laid down. No 7803 *Barcote Manor* was one of the first built, in 1938   [*BR*

"MANOR"
CLASS
4-6-0

BELOW: In BR days some "Manors" had a spell in the West Country where they were often employed as pilot engines on the South Devon banks. No 7812 *Erlestoke Manor* was assisting No 5007 *Rougemont Castle* on the approach to Dainton Tunnel with the 1.20pm Penzance-Paddington, June 29, 1957   [*R. C. Riley*

ABOVE: Hawksworth's "Counties" introduced in 1945 were the most powerful two-cylinder 4-6-0s of the GWR and incorporated some features of his "Modified Halls". The first 19 of the 30 engines built came out without names, but these were fitted from 1946 onwards. In original condition No 1011, later named *County of Chester*, heads an up Weston-super-Mare express near Sonning, 1946   [*M. W. Earley*

"COUNTY"
CLASS
4-6-0

LEFT The "Counties" put in much work north of Wolverhampton, on which route they replaced the "Saints". No 1024 *County of Pembroke* heads a down Chester express north of Shrewsbury in 1953
[*Dr L. N. Owen*

ABOVE: Between 1904 and 1912 Churchward built 40 powerful 4-4-0s for express passenger work, notably on lines over which 4-6-0s were not then allowed. They were not popular owing to rough riding tendencies and all were withdrawn between 1930 and 1933. No 3816 *County of Leicester* near Cheltenham Racecourse with a Torquay-Wolverhampton express, July 24, 1924

[*H. G. W. Household*

BELOW: The last ten, Nos 3821-30, were built in 1911-12 with various modifications including super-heaters and curved front end framing. No 3828 *County of Hereford* stands outside Paddington, June 6, 1931. Nos 3831-9 were 1904 built engines so renumbered in 1912

[*F. J. Agar*

"COUNTY" CLASS 4-4-0

ABOVE: Only nine Churchward mixed traffic 2-8-0s were built, between 1919 and 1923. At first often employed on express passenger work they settled down largely to working overnight express freight trains and were little seen in daylight except on summer Saturdays when they shared express duties with the 4-6-0s. No 4706 leaves Paddington with the 1.25pm Kingswear express, August 29, 1959   [R. C. Riley

MIXED TRAFFIC
2-8-0

BELOW: No 4707 nears Bathampton with a freight for the Westbury line, September 15, 1962
                                [D. H. Ballantyne

Old Oak Common Nocturne—No 4704 stands at the coaling
plant, October 19, 1963   [*C. P. Walker*

Introduced in 1911, the Churchward Moguls proved very successful and eventually over 300 were built. No 5347, in the austere unlined finish of 1918 with brightwork painted over, is at the head of a train of vans built for express fish traffic

[BR

MIXED TRAFFIC
2-6-0

BELOW: The last batch of 20 built in 1932 had side window cabs. No 7335 leaves Mitcheldean Road with the 2.30pm Gloucester-Hereford, June 22, 1963

[G. W. Osborne

RIGHT: No 6399 approaches Dolgelly on the Ruabon-Barmouth line, August 12, 1935. Note the shunt arm of the signal
[*H. F. Wheeller*

BELOW: One of 11 engines of the class sent to France in 1917 for Railway Operating Division service, No 5319 stands at Barmouth on the stock of a summer Saturday through train made up of ER coaches. Another engine to see overseas service, No 5322, has been preserved by the Great Western Society
[*M. D. England*

DEAN

4-4-0s

ABOVE: No 4111 *Marlborough*, in charge of a down stopping train near Tilehurst, was a "Badminton" class engine built in 1898 and withdrawn 30 years later. This class had the curved frames of the older Dean 4-4-0s

[*M. W. Earley*

BELOW: The "Atbara" 4-4-0s were the first straight framed 4-4-0s in 1900, closely followed by the "Bulldogs" from No 3341 upwards. No 4133 *Roberts* approaches Newnham with a Cardiff-Gloucester stopping train, October 1924. Note the oval shaped combined name and number plate on the cab side

[*H. G. W. Household*

ABOVE: Another "Atbara", No 4140, heads the 9.50am Taunton-Birmingham express near Cheltenham Racecourse, July 30, 1924. This engine, formerly named *Adelaide* after the capital of South Australia, lost its name in 1910 on construction of the "Star" Class 4-6-0 *Queen Adelaide* [*H. G. W. Household*

BELOW: "City" Class 4-4-0 No 3702 *Halifax* was one of ten "Atbaras" so rebuilt. The remaining ten "Cities", including the famous *City of Truro*, were built new in 1903. These 20 engines had only a short reign on top express work being superseded by 4-6-0s and all were withdrawn by 1931. Note the non-corridor "Toplight" coaches of 1913 vintage [*M. W. Earley*

ABOVE: From time to time Swindon carried out some extraordinary rebuilds and the "3521" Class 4-4-0s were a classic example, having started life as 0-4-2 or 0-4-4 tank engines. Of the 40 engines of the class, 26 had the small boiler as fitted to the Dean Goods' engines. No 3545 was recorded at Symonds Yat on an Engineer's Inspection Saloon   [*Eric Mason, courtesy A. G. Ellis*

DEAN REBUILT 4-4-0s

BELOW: Large boiler engine No 3525 heads the 3.12pm Kingham-Cheltenham near Charlton Kings, July 5, 1924. The rear three coaches, so obviously superior to the branch line stock at the head of the train, had been slipped at Kingham from the 1.30pm Paddington-Hereford express   [*H. G. W. Household*

No 3309 *Maristow*, standing at Wellington shed, was one of 20 engines rebuilt from "Duke" class. These were Nos 3300-19 and Nos 3320-40 also had curved frames of the type shown   [*W. Potter*

"BULLDOG" CLASS 4-4-0

No 3384 *Swindon*, with an up stopping train on Goring troughs in 1921, was one of 37 4-4-0s to lose their names in 1927 because passengers were alleged to confuse the engine name with the destination of the train!   [*H. J. Patterson Rutherford*

Another engine that lost its name was No 3387 *Reading*, here appropriately standing on Reading shed, September 26, 1925. Note the iron Loco Coal and ash wagons   [*F. J. Agar*

"DUKEDOGS"
AND
"BULLDOGS"

ABOVE: Combination of "Dukedog" and "Duke" near Commins Coch in 1939; the leading engine, No 3204, carries the copper cap chimney as fitted to "Dukedogs" from No 3209 onwards when built and in later years to the surviving "Dukes" [*J. G. Dewing*

BELOW: No 3453 *Seagull* near Swimbridge with a Barnstaple-Taunton train, 1935. Of 45 "Bulldogs" to come into BR hands *Seagull* was one of the last two survivors, being withdrawn in November 1951
[*Donovan E. H. Box*

ABOVE: To replace the veteran "Dukes", the 29 "Dukedogs" were a combination of "Duke" type boilers and cabs on "Bulldog" frames, these 1936-9 rebuilds being similar to the "Duke" *Tre Pol and Pen*, so rebuilt in 1929. Nos 3200-12 originally carried "Earl" names but these were transferred to "Castle" Class 4-6-0s in 1937. In original condition with cast iron chimney, No 3208 *Earl Bathurst* enters Crewe with a train from Wellington   [W. H. C. Kelland

BELOW: The other last "Bulldog", No 3454 *Skylark* approaches Swindon with a down freight, October 24, 1951, about a fortnight before its withdrawal   [J. F. Russell-Smith

"DUKEDOG" 4-4-0

No 3204 heads an evening freight train near Pontdolgoch.   The "Dukedogs" continued to be associated with the Cambrian section until the end of their days.   Two survived until October 1960 and one of these, No 3217, is now preserved on the Bluebell Railway   [*J. G. Dewing*

ABOVE: No. 3286 *Meteor* hauls a down Bramley workman's train near Southcote Junction, 1932. Note the narrow 2,500 gallons capacity tender   [*M. W. Earley*

RIGHT: No 3265 *Tre Pol and Pen*, the 1929 rebuild with straight "Bulldog" frames, at Aberystwyth shed, August 5, 1935   [*F. M. Butterfield*

"DUKE"

4-4-0

No 3254 *Cornubia* pauses at Kingsworthy on the Didcot, Newbury & Southampton line, May 18, 1935. At the time the DN&S was largely the preserve of "Dukes", Dean Goods and MSWJ 2-4-0s
[*N. Shepherd*

"DUKE" CLASS 4-4-0

In post-war years "Duke" class No 9083 *Comet* stands at Woodhay. This engine retained the original narrow cab with outside springs until withdrawal in 1950. It was renumbered from 3283 at the end of 1946. By this time "Dukes" were rare on the DN&S and "Bulldog" 4-4-0s and Collett 0-6-0s were largely used
[*G. L. Hoare*

52

ABOVE: The Didcot, Newbury & Southampton Railway provided a north to south connection as did the MSWJR, but while the latter remained independent until 1923, the DN&S was always reliant on the GWR to work its trains. Both were largely completed in the 1880s and closed in the early 1960s. Collett 0-6-0s took over much of the train working in the thirties and this busy scene at Upton & Blewbury shows No 2282 on a Didcot-Southampton train crossing a northbound freight, pannier tank hauled, 1938 [*M. W. Earley*

DN&S LINE

BELOW: For a time from 1957 the preserved 4-4-0 *City of Truro* had a regular duty over the line. Here it passes Shawford Junction on the former LSW Southampton main line with a train from Didcot. This engine was said to have attained 102.3mph on a Plymouth Ocean Liner express in 1904. It is now in Swindon Museum

[*L. Elsey*

ABOVE: Old Newbury at the turn of the Century, with a "3232" class 2-4-0 heading an up passenger train. The overall roof was added in 1882 when improvements were carried out largely at the expense of the DN&S Railway. Note the informative station nameboard typical of GWR junction stations   [H. J. Patterson Rutherford

BELOW: Newbury in 1920 with Armstrong Goods 0-6-0 No 696 in charge of a down freight train. The four track rebuilding took place in 1909-10 as a result of increased traffic to the West following opening of the Castle Cary-Taunton direct line   [H. J. Patterson Rutherford

ABOVE: Worcester shed in 1894 with Dean and Armstrong Goods 0-6-0s and saddle tanks predominating. Note that in those days the Dean Goods had domes forward on the boiler and round topped smokeboxes, contrasting to the Belpaire fireboxes familiar later and which were the cause of rebuilding of the saddle tanks to pannier tanks
[L&GRP

BELOW: A less busy scene 60 years later—the buildings are little altered. The shed yard now contains 4-6-0s, 2-8-0s, 2-6-2 tanks and 0-6-0 pannier tanks. In the foreground No 6864 *Dymock Grange* *[R. C. Riley*

ABOVE: There were over 300 of the Armstrong Goods engines and some of them had a lifespan of 60 years or more. No 1111, built in 1871, was on a down goods near Warwick in 1928, the year of its withdrawal   [L&GRP

RIGHT: There were 260 Dean Goods 0-6-0s built between 1883 and 1897 and some of them served overseas in both World Wars. No 2349 of 1884 was recorded in ROD livery at Outreau in Northern France November 1918
[W. H. C. Kelland

LEFT: A curious conversion between 1907 and 1910 was of 20 Dean Goods 0-6-0s to 2-6-2 tanks, largely for use in the Birmingham area. They were all withdrawn in the early thirties. No 3915 pauses at Radley, June 1930
[G. C. Allen

DEAN GOODS
0-6-0

ABOVE: No 2550, built in 1897, heads northbound light engine through Birmingham Snow Hill, February 20, 1939. The following year it became No 153 of the War Department and went to France. After the war it was one of several Dean Goods to be sent to China where it may still survive—who knows? [N. Shepherd

LEFT: No 2354, an 1884 engine, survived into BR days and was one of a few of the class to carry boilers with top feed. It was recorded on a freight train bound for Moat Lane at Talyllyn Junction, May 3, 1951
[R. C. Riley

BELOW: No 2526 was recorded near Long Ashton on a Bristol-Wells train in pre-war days. In 1940 it became WD No 132 and was last recorded five years later carrying Polish numbers in Eastern Germany [G. H. Soole

ABOVE: The Collett 0-6-0s were introduced in 1930 and 120 were built over the next 18 years. No 2279 heads a northbound freight up Hatton bank, April 20, 1957   [*R. C. Riley*

COLLETT 0-6-0

BELOW: No 3203 pauses at Newent with the last train from Gloucester to Ledbury, July 11, 1959. Another 1946 built engine, No 3205, is preserved at Bridgnorth   [*W. Potter*

ABOVE: The "Aberdares" earned their name from their original association with the working of coal trains from Aberdare. Built between 1900 and 1907 they were still regularly used 30 years later on Loco Coal trains from Rogerstone to Old Oak Common. No 2662 was recorded on the LMS & GWR Joint Line near Frodsham with a freight train from Birkenhead, July 1939   [Dr Ian C. Allen

"ABERDARE" CLASS 2-6-0

BELOW: No 2673 heads north past Cheltenham Malvern Road with a mineral train from South Wales, August 1945.   On shed in the background was No 2638 with a broken crankpin; it was never repaired and was withdrawn the following month. The last "Aberdare" survived until 1949.   Most of them in later years, including those illustrated, had tenders from withdrawn ROD 2-8-0s   [W. Potter

LEFT: Churchward's first 2-8-0 goods engine came out in 1903, the first of its kind in the country, and by 1919 there were 84 in service. Between 1938 and 1942 this total was doubled by new construction. One of the later engines, No 3821, takes the Worcester avoiding line at Tunnel Junction with empty mineral wagons for South Wales, via Hereford, April 15, 1956   [*R. C. Riley*

RIGHT: No 2874 pounds up Sapperton bank with a freight train banked in the rear by a large 2-6-2 tank. Built in 1918 this engine never acquired outside steam pipes to the cylinders. No 2818 of this class is preserved at Bristol but not yet on public display   [*G. F. Heiron*

28xx CLASS 2-8-0

LEFT: Another of the later engines, No 3846, heads an up mineral train from South Wales at Wootton Bassett, September 18, 1955
[*R. C. Riley*

ABOVE: Between 1917 and 1919 over 500 2-8-0s of Great Central Railway design were built for the Railway Operating Division, only some of which went overseas. The GWR bought 100 of them, of which 50 were scrapped between 1927 and 1931, the rest remaining in traffic until 1946-58. ROD 1897 was recorded at Reading shed in 1925 and later became GWR No 3034. At left is 4-4-0 No 3528   [F. J. Agar

ROD 2-8-0

BELOW: In later condition with GWR boiler mountings No 3017 heads a heavy freight train near Hatherley Junction, Cheltenham, May 1, 1937
[H. G. W. Household

HEAVY FREIGHT TANKS

ABOVE: The 51xx Class 2-6-2 tanks were maids of all work and much used on passenger trains, notably in the Midlands. Severn Tunnel Junction had a few, together with the larger 31xx Class, and these were largely used piloting heavy freight trains through the tunnel. No 5118 was on a local freight from Bristol, passing Patchway and heading towards the tunnel   [G. H. Soole

LEFT: The 42xx Class 2-8-0 tanks introduced in 1910 were almost entirely allocated to South and West Wales hauling trains from the coalfields to the main line, and to ports and steelworks.   No 4283 was recorded outside Swindon Works   [J. P. Mullett

RIGHT: The 72xx Class 2-8-2 tanks of 1934-40 were rebuilt from 2-8-0 tanks with additional coal and water capacity for main line work.   No 7236 in post-war livery stands on Leamington shed, June 10, 1946   [R. C. Riley

ABOVE: All GW freight vehicles had code names to denote their type. This bogie well wagon carrying the 1925 built replica of the 1838 engine *North Star* is a "Crocodile H" [*BR*

ROLLING STOCK

The use of old clerestory coaches in departmental service was widespread and an eight compartment vehicle similar to that shown has been preserved at Didcot by the Great Western Society, although much restoration work is required. Some GW goods brake vans have also been preserved [*J. L. Smith Collection*

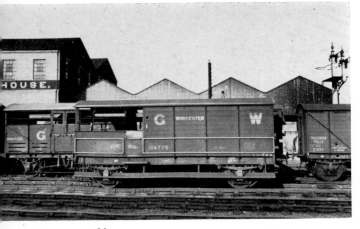

A typical GW 20 ton goods brake, code-name "Toad", branded as working from Worcester [*HMRS Collection*

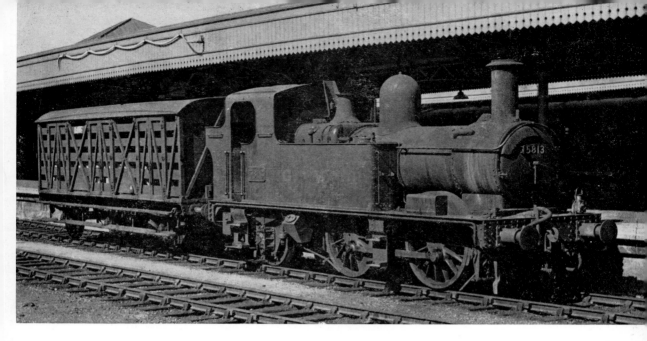

ABOVE: 0-4-2 tank No 5813 at Bristol Temple Meads with a "High Siphon" van, much used for milk churn traffic
[*J. P. Wilson*

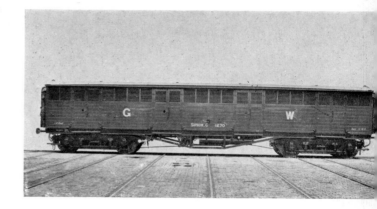

The largest vans were classified "Siphon G" and these were very well known, although of several varieties [*BR*

ROLLING STOCK

A "Fruit" van, vacuum fitted for passenger train use, with an end-door "Siphon C" van for milk traffic at right
[*HMRS Collection*

65

ABOVE: 2-8-0 No 2867, in original condition with built-up chimney, heads a train of 50 iron 20-ton coal wagons. These were much used to convey South Wales coal traffic   [*BR*

ROLLING STOCK

There were many varieties of "Iron Mink" built over a period of about 25 years until 1912.   A few survive, and many ended their days providing storage accommodation in goods yards, either on or off wheels   [*BR*

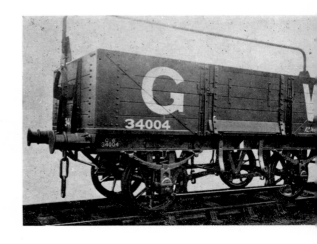

A typical GW 12 tons open wagon with tarpaulin attachment   [*BR*

ABOVE: Covered goods vans of 10 and 12 ton capacity. That on the left carries a plate "RETURN TO GWR NOT COMMON USER". Both vehicles are vacuum fitted. At extreme left a later type of 10 ton van   [*HMRS Collection*

ROLLING STOCK

A Large Cattle Wagon with lettering on the ends as well as on the sides. A partition placed against the S mark reduced accommodation to that of a Small Cattle Wagon, the M to that of a medium. The farmer only got what he was prepared to pay for!   [*BR*

Most shunting yards of any importance had their Shunter's Truck. This example was at Westbury   [*R. C. Riley*

2-4-0 "Metro Tank" No 3570 in Old Oak Common shed with condensing apparatus for use on through trains over Metropolitan Railway lines [*LPC*

LONDON SUBURBAN

2-6-2 tank No 4509 on down empty coaches near Westbourne Park. These small 2-6-2 tanks were quite common in the London area until 1930 when standard panneirs replaced them. In 1933 the last two left, transferred to Truro, and the class did not return to the London area until shortly before their withdrawal 30 years later [*J. L. Smith Collection*

In post-war livery, No 5410 stands at Ealing Broadway on the Greenford railmotor service, a Central Line train in the background. The 54xx tanks spent most of their life in the London area. The trailer car is No 54 built in this form in 1908 [*J. L. Smith Collection*

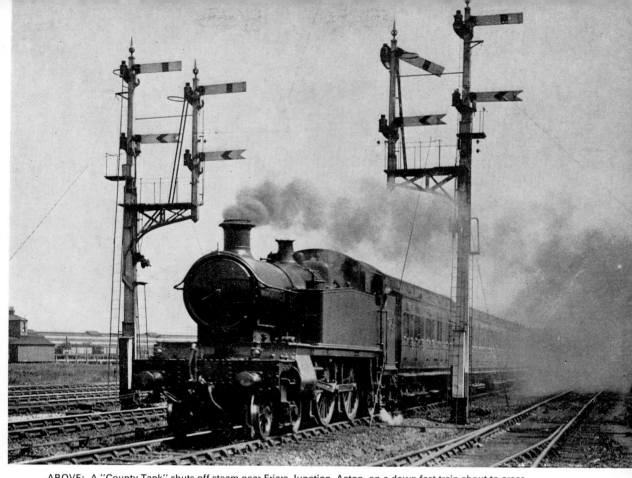

ABOVE: A "County Tank" shuts off steam near Friars Junction, Acton, on a down fast train about to cross from main to relief line. These 4-4-2 tanks were the mainstay of the London outer suburban trains from 1905 until displaced by 61xx 2-6-2 tanks in 1931, the last "County Tank" being withdrawn four years later
[BR

BELOW: Then less than three months old, No 6100 heads a down fast train out of Paddington, June 13, 1931. These 2-6-2 tanks remained until the end of steam
[F. J. Agar

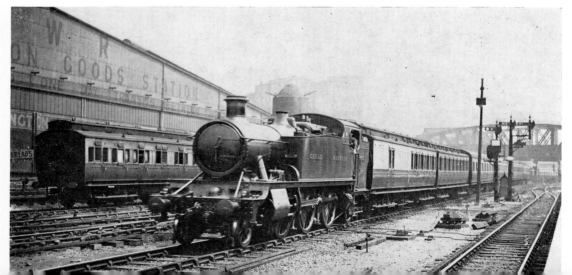

ABOVE: "Modified Hall" 4-6-0 No 6966 *Witchingham Hall* heads a freight from the Oxford line round the loop towards Foxhall Junction, and thence to Swindon.   To the right of the signal the one time entry to the extensive Ordnance Depot sidings, May 19, 1962 [*D. A. Anderson*

DIDCOT

BELOW: No 7029 *Clun Castle* heads a down special train past Foxhall Junction, April 3, 1965. This engine worked the last scheduled steam train out of Paddington on June 11, 1965, and has since been privately preserved   [*D. A. Anderson*

ABOVE: SR Bulleid Pacific No 34051 *Winston Churchill* runs light to the shed to turn after bringing in the Bournemouth-Newcastle express, August 29, 1964. Among engines on shed are 2-6-2 tank No 6111 and 4-6-0s 7014 *Caerhays Castle* and 6923 *Croxteth Hall*   [*C. P. Walker*

OXFORD

BELOW: 0-6-0 pannier tank No 9654 crosses part of the Oxford Canal to the north of the station, with the wooden engine shed at left, June 9, 1962   [*D. A. Anderson*

ABOVE: Large 2-6-2 tank No 3176 near Warwick with a Leamington-Birmingham train. Of all the classes of GWR 2-6-2 tank Nos 3150-90, and later rebuilds Nos 3100-4 were the largest   [L&GRP

BIRMINGHAM SUBURBAN

ABOVE: Small 2-6-2 tank No 5524 heads an up Leamington local near Bentley Heath. The four coach local sets of 1925 vintage remained on these services until displaced by diesel multiple units [W. L. Good

BELOW: "Metro" 2-4-0 tank No 3563 at Stratford-upon-Avon with a train from Leamington, 1928
[L&GRP

ABOVE: 2-6-2 tank No 5166 leaves Stratford-upon-Avon for Birmingham, April 21, 1957. The 51xx 2-6-2 tanks predominated on local services in the West Midlands   [R. C. Riley

BELOW: 0-6-2 tank No 6609 heads an up local on Rowington troughs, near Lapworth   [T. E. Williams

LEFT: 2-6-2 tank No 5192 enters Snow Hill with an up excursion, August 3, 1935. An Open Third 1905 "Dreadnought" coach similar to the leading vehicle is preserved by the Great Western Society at Didcot
[H. F. Wheeller

BIRMINGHAM

BELOW: No 6001 *King Edward VII* leaves Snow Hill station with the 1.10pm Paddington-Birkenhead, March 21, 1960. While electrification works were taking place on the LMR main line out of Euston passenger traffic to and from Birmingham was concentrated on the Paddington line, which had an hourly service. Now the wheel has turned full circle, Birmingham New Street has been rebuilt and Snow Hill virtually closed [R. C. Riley

WOLVERHAMPTON

ABOVE: No 4944 *Middleton Hall* enters Wolverhampton with the Birkenhead-Bournemouth train, August 23, 1936
[*S. W. Baker*

BELOW: No 6000 *King George V* stands in the up platform with a Paddington express, 1961. This engine has been preserved by BR and is now in the custody of Messrs H. P. Bulmer Ltd at their Hereford cider factory
[*M. Pope*

WELLINGTON SHED

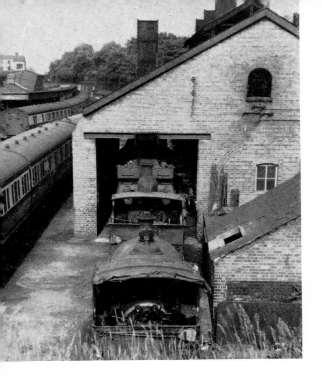

LEFT: The engine shed at Wellington provides a good example of a small brick built GWR shed. It supplied motive power for local trains to Wolverhampton and Shrewsbury, the line to Market Drayton and Crewe, and the branch to Much Wenlock and Craven Arms. On the back road behind the shed stand an open cab 0-6-0 saddle tank and a similar pannier tank
[G. H. W. Clifford

RIGHT: Wellington was the last home of the "Barnum" 2-4-0s, of which 20 were built in 1889. The last two were withdrawn in 1937, one of them being No 3210, seen outside the shed, August 3, 1935
[H. F. Wheeller

LEFT: Another glimpse of No 3210 on Wellington shed, with a Siphon Van in the sidings at right
[H. F. Wheeller

"Stella" Class 2-4-0 No 3204 at the coal stage, April 28, 1922. Like the "Barnums" these engines were used on trains to Crewe. No 3204 was withdrawn in 1929 but the last survivor, No 3518, was at Wellington until 1932

[*H. G. W. Household*

"Barnum" 2-4-0 No 3223 on the turntable at the north end of the shed yard beyond the coal stage   [*W. Potter*

As archaic as some of the shed's occupants was this old broad gauge coach body used as a store behind the shed August 3, 1935

[*H. F. Wheeller*

ABOVE: The vogue for steam railmotors, which started on the continent, began here in 1903 with the GWR among the pioneers.   They were first used between Stone-house and Chalford, on which service is Railmotor No 4 standing in Stroud station about 1904   [A. K. Pope Collection

STEAM RAILMOTORS

BELOW: Railmotor No 70, built in 1906, about to leave Southall for Brentford in 1931.   The last of the GW steam railmotors was withdrawn four years later.   Most of the carriage portions were converted to trailer cars for motor train use

[Dr Ian C. Allen

RAILMOTOR
TRAINS

LEFT: 0-4-2 tank No 527 at Staines sandwiched between two trailer cars, the nearer of which, No 117, was converted from Railmotor No 21 in 1920. The severe outline with matchboard sides was confined to the first 26 railmotors built in 1903-4   [J. L. Smith Collection

ABOVE: A typical Plymouth area railmotor train with six-coupled tank No 1284 between two pairs of 70ft suburban type trailers near Laira in 1925. The leading vehicle is No 135, converted from Railmotor No 44, built in 1905   [F. J. Agar

LEFT: Between 1895 and 1898 when main line coaches were built with clerestory roofs several branch line coaches were built without this feature. Some converted for motor train use were known as the "Clifton Down" type, having replaced railmotors on this service. 0-4-2 tank No 526 propels two such coaches and trails a horse box near Reading West

[H. J. Patterson Rutherford

RAILMOTOR
TRAINS

ABOVE: Between 1929 and 1933 40 new railmotor trailers were built. Of these Car No 178 spent most of its life working between Ruabon, Dolgelley and Barmouth. It is here seen at Ruabon with 0-4-2 tank No 4828 in 1935. It survived to be taken over by the LMR and became a most unlikely vehicle in departmental use at Wolverton Works, whence it was rescued for the Severn Valley Railway Preservation Society

[H. F. Wheeller

BELOW: 0-6-0 tank No 6429, built in 1935, with compartment type railmotor No 1670, one of four such vehicles built in 1939 and numbered in the ordinary carriage series. The train is leaving Ardley for Princes Risborough, November 10, 1959

[D. M. C. Hepburne Scott

ABOVE: Early to foresee the possibilities of diesel cars, the GWR built 38 such vehicles between 1934 and 1942. Car No 12 was recorded at Worcester Shrub Hill, August 22, 1936   [S. W. Baker

DIESEL
RAILCARS

RIGHT: Car No 17 was built for express parcels' service in the London area and is seen passing West Drayton in 1937. It was later replaced by Car No 34, which could haul vans if required, and ended its career in the Birmingham district   [W. H. C. Kelland

BELOW: Car No 32 of the later series fitted with drawgear stands below a pleasant cast iron footbridge at Chipping Norton, October 9, 1954   [S. C. Nash

ABOVE: Between 1870 and 1881 Swindon turned out over 250 outside framed saddle tanks of the "1076" class, not unlike the older Wolverhampton "1016" class. From 1911 onwards most engines were fitted with Belpaire boilers, hence pannier tanks replaced the original saddle tanks. No 1650 pauses at Dulverton after taking water before returning to Exeter with a pick-up goods train

[W. H. C. Kelland]

VINTAGE PANNIER TANKS

BELOW: Two "2021" class engines provide a contrast between saddle tank and pannier tank. 0-6-0ST No 2028 and 0-6-0PT No 2052 were recorded in Shrewsbury shed, August 4, 1935. They were built in 1897 and 1898 respectively

[H. F. Wheeller]

ABOVE: Only six of the "1366" class engines were built, in 1934. They replaced older engines at Swindon Wagon Works but soon became more familiar on the Weymouth Harbour Tramway. On replacement by diesels the three Weymouth engines were transferred to Wadebridge, where they took over Wenford mineral line duties from the LSWR Beattie 2-4-0 tanks. No 1369 is now preserved at Buckfastleigh. No 1366 was in charge of a Channel Islands' boat train at Weymouth Quay, 1949 *[Donovan E. H. Box*

DISTINCTIVE PANNIERS

BELOW: Two remarkable pannier tanks were built at Swindon in 1901, Nos 17 *Cyclops* and 18 *Steropes*. They were basically "850" class pannier tanks with domeless boilers to allow lowering of the crane jib, the crane being accommodated on the rear bogie. A third engine, No 16 *Hercules* was built in 1921. Nos 16 and 18 were always at Swindon Works, but No 17 was recorded at Wolverhampton Stafford Road Works, where it spent all but the last two years of its life. All were withdrawn in 1936 *[BR*

ABOVE: Between 1929 and 1950 no less than 863 57xx Class pannier tanks were built, one of the most numerous classes of engine in the country. 1931 built No 8745 passes Grange Court Junction with a Lydney-Gloucester freight, October 17, 1964. A few of these low cab engines survive in London Transport ownership

[D. R. G. Nowell

BELOW: Starting with No 8750 in 1933 later engines were fitted with a larger cab No 9605, a 1945 built engine, propels its nominal load into the sidings at Swindon Junction, while on pilot duty. Note the calling-on arm in the "off" position

[R. C. Riley

ABOVE: Nos 9700-10 were fitted with condensing apparatus to enable them to work over the Metropolitan lines to the GWR depot at Smithfield.   They were also much used on empty stock trains in and out of Paddington.   No 9709, still sporting GWR livery approaches Kensington with a van train, August 18, 1956

[R. C. Riley

ANNIERS

BELOW: Ten outside cylindered short wheelbase pannier tanks were built in 1949 and several were used on Paddington empty stock trains.   No 1505 was recorded in Old Oak Common carriage depot with two Plymouth Ocean Liner saloons, some of which have been preserved.   Three 15xx engines survived at Coventry Colliery until the end of 1969 and two may saved for the Severn Valley Railway   [R. C. Riley

LEFT: Small 2-6-2 tank No 4410 rounds the coast near Carbis Bay with the "Cornish Riviera Express" through coaches for St Ives. Only 11 of these engines were built between 1904 and 1906
[Dr Ian C. Allen

CORNISH BRANCHES

BELOW: 45xx class 2-6-2 tank No 4552 climbs through the Luxulyan Valley with a Par-Newquay train, July 9, 1955. These were lively little engines and the first 75, built between 1906 and 1924, had smaller coal and water capacity than the later engines so being lighter and more suitable for branch line work
[R. C. Riley

RIGHT: 0-6-0 pannier tank No 5771 leaves Clifton Down with a train for Avonmouth　　[*G. H. Soole*

BRISTOL BRANCHES

BELOW: One of the later 45xx engines with larger side tanks, No 5508 crosses Pensford viaduct on the 2.53pm Bristol-Radstock-Frome train, March 14, 1955　　　　　　　[*D. H. Ballantyne*

WEYMOUTH

LEFT: "Duke" Class 4-4-0 No 3270 *Earl of Devon* approaches Weymouth with a down passenger train. The engine shed is visible in the background. The $168\frac{1}{4}$ milepost at left is a reminder of the original route from Paddington, via Chippenham and Trowbridge. The later more direct route via Newbury was not available until the opening from Patney & Chirton to Westbury in 1900, reducing the mileage to 154   [L&GRP

ABOVE: The Weymouth Harbour Tramway was worked by a variety of tank engines including between 1926 and 1939, two 0-6-0 saddle tanks from the Burry Port & Gwendraeth Valley Railway, Nos 2194 *Kidwelly* and 2195 *Cwm Mawr*. The latter was recorded at Weymouth Quay, July 9, 1935   [F. J. Agar]

LEFT: Two engines associated with the Tramway from 1881 until displaced by the BPGV saddle tanks were former Bristol & Exeter Railway 0-6-0 tanks No 1376/77, of which the former heads a Channel Islands Boat express along Commercial Road   [A. G. Ellis]

ABOVE: "517" class 0-4-2 tank No 562 of 1869 vintage in charge of a Winchcombe-Cheltenham railmotor train near Cheltenham Racecourse, July 24, 1924
[H. G. W. Household

COTSWOLD
BRANCHES

RIGHT: "Metro" 2-4-0 tank No 628 of 1871 vintage with a charming period train on the Cheltenham-Kingham service near Charlton Kings, April 5, 1924.   A Dean 40ft Guards Van similar to the leading vehicle is preserved on the Severn Valley line
[H. G. W. Household

BELOW: In BR days 2-8-2 tank No 7214 passes Hayles Abbey Halt on the Honeybourne-Cheltenham line with a ballast train.   Note the waiting shed provided when the halt opened in 1928 was more austere than the earlier pagoda type
[R. C. Riley

0-6-0 pannier tank No 7436 pauses to take water at Witney with an Oxford-Fairford train, May 14, 1951. This was among the last preserves of the Metro Tanks, withdrawn two years earlier. Note the standard GW water column and ornate lamp. The Fairford branch closed in 1962
[*R. C. Riley*

Another pannier tank, No 2098, at Watlington with a train for Princes Risborough, June 6, 1934. The trailer coach was kept in the shed at left, the branch engine standing in the open overnight or at weekends
[*F. M. Butterfield*

The Watlington branch had charming little stations, of which Aston Rowant was an example. Passenger traffic was withdrawn in 1957 but the first station on the branch, Chinnor, is still served by freight trains
[*R. C. Riley*

FOREST
OF
DEAN

The Forest of Dean once had an intensive network of lines, primarily for mineral traffic.   In lined green livery, No 5417 was on a Railway Enthusiasts Club Special at the Severn & Wye Railway's Coleford terminus, April 20, 1958.   Leading coach is compartment Trailer No 254 converted in 1955 from a Brake Third 20 years older; at rear a BR built trailer of conventional GW open type
[R. C. Riley

No 1623 was one of a class of 70 small pannier tanks built in BR days to replace older similar engines. It is approaching Ruspidge Halt on a 1 in 58 gradient with the 2.58pm Newnham-Cinderford, May 15, 1957, a year before passenger traffic ceased   [D. H. Ballantyne

No 3675 near Bilson Junction with Cinderford branch freight, October 11, 1965.   Note the calling-on signal
[W. Potter

ABOVE: The Cleobury Mortimer & Ditton Priors Light Railway, 13 miles in length, was a late arrival on the railway scene in 1908 and was to have only 13 years of independent existence. Motive power was provided by two Manning Wardle 0-6-0 saddle tanks of which *Cleobury* (GWR No 28) is seen on a passenger train

[*M. D. England*

CLEOBURY MORTIMER
& DITTON PRIORS

BELOW: Both engines were rebuilt as pannier tanks by the GWR and in this form survived until 1953-4. Passenger traffic ceased in 1938, but freight traffic survived for nearly 30 years longer thanks to construction of a Naval Ordnance Depot in 1939. In rebuilt form No 29 (originally *Burwarton*) heads a freight train, September 1938, the crane being for timber loading

[*S. H. Pearce Higgins*

MIDLAND & SOUTH WESTERN JUNCTION

The MSWJ provided a useful cross country route between Cheltenham and Southampton by virtue of running powers over the GWR at its north end and the LSWR at the south.   In its heyday its smart red engines and trains were a sight to behold.   Its most modern engines were nine 4-4-0s built between 1905 and 1914, the last two of which carried a separate top feed dome.   Here is one of these, MSWJ No 4 (later GWR 1122) piloting No 3559 on the 10.24am Southampton-Cheltenham, near Charlton Kings, February 14, 1924.   Note the LNWR through coach to Liverpool behind the MSWJ coaches, bought secondhand from the MR   [*H. G. W. Household*

ABOVE: The MSWJ had ten 0-6-0s built by Beyer Peacock 1899-1902 primarily for goods traffic but often seen on passenger trains. No 1008 heads the 8.0am Andover Junction-Cheltenham near Hatherley Junction, July 2, 1925. The GWR rebuilt these engines with standard taper boilers. Note the Low Siphon van   [H. G. W. Household

BELOW: MSWJ 4-4-0 No 1 as GWR No 1119 at Andover Junction shed, August 31, 1934. This was one of three of the class not to receive a GWR taper boiler. The LSWR and MSWJ sheds were side by side here, and in later years only the former shed was used   [N. Shepherd

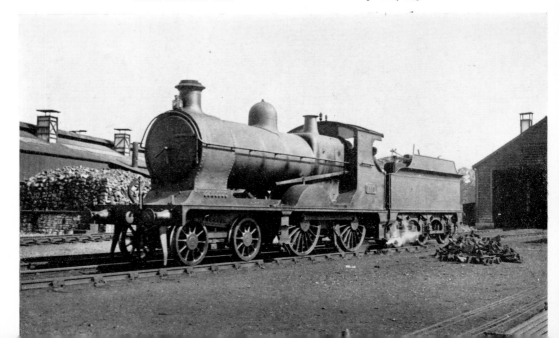

ABOVE: After grouping the GWR quickly drafted "Duke" 4-4-0s to the line to replace MSWJ engines sent to Swindon for reboilering.   No 3273 *Mounts Bay* was working the 2.40pm Andover Junction-Cheltenham, composed of MSWJ coaches, near Charlton Kings, July 8, 1924   [*H. G. W. Household*

BELOW: Withdrawal of the MSWJ 4-4-0s was completed in 1938 by which time "Dukedogs" and "Bulldogs" were in charge of the through trains.   No 3209 *Earl of Radnor* was at Andover Junction shed, May 16, 1937.   This engine lost its name the following month, transferred to "Castle" 4-6-0 No 5052   [*F. M. Butterfield*

CAMBRIAN RAILWAYS

ABOVE LEFT: The Cambrian Railways system was the largest to be absorbed by the GWR in 1922 with over 300 miles of line. Its passenger engines included 22 4-4-0s built between 1893 and 1904, one of which was destroyed in the 1921 Abermule disaster. No 1091, shown here, spent the latter years of its life working from Machynlleth on the Cambrian Coast line, until withdrawn in 1930 [J. L. Smith Collection

LEFT: Like the MSWJ 0-6-0s those of the Cambrian were often found in passenger service. 15 of the Large Belpaire Goods engines were built and all but four survived to enter BR ownership. No 896 approaches Barmouth with a train from Dovey Junction, August 1935 [H. F. Wheeller

LEFT: The attractive 2-4-0 tank No 1308 *Lady Margaret* was built for the Liskeard & Looe Railway in 1902 and transferred to the Cambrian Section 20 years later. It shared duties on the Tanat Valley Light Railway with the Cambrian 2-4-0 tanks and survived until 1948 [J. L. Smith Collection

RIGHT: Summit point of the main line is the impressive rock cutting at Talerddig, between Carno and Llanbryn-mair. With a depth of 120ft it was the deepest of its kind on construction in 1861. Churchward Mogul No 7320 storms towards the summit with a summer Saturday through train in 1963 [M. Pope

VALE
OF
RHEIDOL

Steam survives on BRs remaining narrow gauge system, nearly 12 miles of 1ft 11½in gauge from Aberystwyth to Devils Bridge. It started life as an independent concern in 1902, but was absorbed by the Cambrian Railways in 1913 and so became part of the GWR nine years later. One of the original engines survives, No 9, but Nos 7 and 8 were built to the original design in 1923. No 7 *Owain Glyndwr* is seen in the BR rail blue livery acquired in 1968

[*M. Pope*

SOUTH
WALES

The GWR built 200 0-6-2 tanks primarily for service in South Wales. No 5654 approaches Caerphilly with a Cardiff-Rhymney train, September 24, 1956. The Rhymney Railway favoured the somersault signal as did several of the Cardiff Valleys lines   [E. R. Mountford]

Most modern passenger engines of the Rhymney Railway were four 0-6-2 tanks of 1921, of which No 78 stands at Rhymney shed, April 20, 1935. This engine was not reboilered by the GWR until 1949 and survived until 1955
[F. M. Butterfield]

No 38 was another 1921 built Rhymney Railway engine, primarily for freight work. It heads D8 freight from Cardiff Docks to Rhymney near Wernddu, Caerphilly, October 24, 1955. Never reboilered by the GWR this engine survived until 1957   [E. R. Mountford]

ABOVE: The South Wales scene is one of contrasts, much pleasant scenery but industry never far away. A Taff Vale Railway Class 04 0-6-2 tank, No 282, of 1908, heads an Aberdare train near Pontcynon, June 20, 1949
[*W. H. G. Boot*

SOUTH
WALES

RIGHT: No 364, a Taff Vale A class 0-6-2 tank heads a southbound coal train near Penrhos Junction. As with No 282 above it has been rebuilt by the GWR. Trains in the Cardiff Valleys carried distinctive target letters, CP denoting Caerphilly May 12, 1952   [*R. C. Riley*

ABOVE: Rebuilt Taff Vale 0-6-2 tank No 312 stands in Barry station on a Vale of Glamorgan line train to Bridgend, June, 3, 1953   [*E. R. Mountford*

SOUTH
WALES

BELOW: Barry Railway 0-6-0 saddle tank No 742 at Swindon shed, September 11, 1932. This engine had just been sold out of service returning to South Wales to shunt at Treorchy Colliery for a further 30 years
[*F. M. Butterfield*

GREAT WESTERN SOCIETY

Most impressive record of GWR preservation is that of the Great Western Society which cares for several locomotives and rolling stock items at various centres. The main depot is at Didcot and Open Days have been held from time to time there and on the nearby Wallingford branch by courtesy of BR. Beautifully restored 0-4-2 tank No 1466 and BR built Trailer No 231 leave Cholsey for Wallingford, September 21, 1968
[*S. C. Nash*

ABOVE: One of the last 61xx 2-6-2 tanks overhauled at Swindon was No 6106 seen at Brimscombe shed, September 26, 1964, on Sapperton banking duty. This engine is now preserved by the GWS at Didcot [D. M. Ballantyne]

BELOW: No 7808 Cookham Manor is preserved by the GWS and accommodated by the Dowty RPS at Ashchurch. It is here leaving Whitehouse Farm Tunnel, near Beaconsfield, with a GWS Special from Birmingham to Taplow, September 17, 1966 [M. Pope]

ABOVE: The Severn Valley Railway opened in 1862 to provide a useful link between Shrewsbury and Worcester. Passenger traffic was withdrawn in the year following the line's centenary, when the centre part of the line between Buildwas and Alvely was closed to all traffic. 2-6-2 tank No 5518 heads the 5.30pm Shrewsbury-Kidderminster at Bridgnorth, July 24, 1954 *[W. A. Camwell*

SEVERN VALLEY LINE

LEFT: Imposing station frontage at Bridgnorth, now the centre of operations of the Severn Valley Railway Preservation Society, which is preserving the five miles thence to Hampton Loade. A number of interesting locomotives, coaches and wagons have been acquired, and a considerable amount of work carried out on buildings and track. Future plans envisage the Southward extension to Bewdley and possibly as far as Kidderminster *[D. C. Williams*

ABOVE: The beautifully restored Collett 0-6-0 No 3205 at Bridgnorth, showing detail of the equally well restored cast-iron footbridge   [D. C. Williams

BELOW: No 3205 heads a works' train out of Bridgnorth, the leading coach being a Third Brake of 1920 City stock built for service over the Metropolitan Railway, two of which found their way to Bridgnorth after use on miners' trains in South Wales   [M. Pope

ABOVE: 0-4-2 tank No 1427 at Ashburton station, a year before the passenger service ceased in 1958. Freight traffic was withdrawn four years later when a group of business men began negotiations to save the line

[R. C. Riley

DART VALLEY LINE

BELOW: Another 0-4-2 tank, No 1470, pauses at Buckfastleigh with the Ashburton-Totnes goods. Buckfastleigh is now the centre from which the preservation company operates, the sidings filled to capacity with preserved GW engines and coaches

[J. A. Coiley

Although special trains had run on previous occasions the official re-opening took place on April 5, 1969, when 0-6-0 pannier tank No 6412 flanked on either side by two trailer cars provided a heavily patronised service over the Totnes-Buckfastleigh section. No 6412 is here seen leaving Staverton Bridge for Buckfastleigh, April 13, 1969
[*P. W. Gray*

ABOVE: In steam days the works yard outside the main erecting shop at Swindon was a bustling scene of activity viewed with great interest from the passing train. Nowadays it seems a dead place and one is left to suppose that modern diesel locomotives are sneaked in surreptitiously by dead of night! Prominent engines in this post-war view include 2-6-2 tanks Nos 4528 and 5512 and 2-8-2 tank No 7247 [BR

SWINDON WORKS

BELOW: Churchward installed the stationary testing plant at Swindon as early as 1902 but its busiest period was probably in the years following nationalisation. The "Castle" 4-6-0 standing on the plant is No 111 *Viscount Churchill*, a 1924 rebuild incorporating parts of *The Great Bear* [BR

ABOVE: No 5005 *Manorbier Castle* takes water on Fox's Wood troughs, Keynsham with the 1pm Cardiff-Brighton train, May 6, 1953. The train is composed of SR stock
[*W. N. Lockett*

TRAINS ON TROUGHS

BELOW: No 4910 *Blaisdon Hall*, as built in 1929 with 3,500 gallon tender, heads a down stopping train on Ruislip troughs in 1933. The two "Low Siphons" leading seem to be having a drenching
[*Dr Ian C. Allen*

ABOVE: Except on the South Devon banks and other steeply graded lines double-heading on the GWR was an uncommon sight.   In this case No 6987 *Shervington Hall* was being worked back to its home shed and pilots No 5037 *Monmouth Castle* on the 1.45pm Paddington-Hereford near Southall, August 10, 1957   [*R. C. Riley*

DOUBLE HEADED

LEFT: On some lines it was laid down that the train engine should be coupled ahead of the assisting engine as in this case with No 5972 *Olton Hall* and 0-6-0PT No 7715 heading into the hills north of St Blazey, July 9, 1955.   The 11 coach train was the summer service Fridays Only 12.5pm Empty Diners from Paddington to Newquay. An 0-6-0PT No 1664 was providing banking assistance at the rear   [*R. C. Riley*

STEAM BY NIGHT

ABOVE: No 5026 *Criccieth Castle*, with double chimney, stands at the head of the 7.10pm Wolverhampton train at Paddington in 1962   [*M. Pope*

RIGHT: Another double chimney engine, the preserved No 7029 *Clun Castle* stands outside its new home on the former coal stage at Tyseley.   The fire is being dropped after a successful Open Day, September 29, 1968   [*J. R. Carter*

ABOVE: No 5000 *Launceston Castle,* built in 1926, was once regularly used on the "Cheltenham Flyer" with its 65min schedule for the 77¼ miles from Swindon to London.   In its last days, as grimy as it had once been well groomed, *Launceston Castle* pauses at Ledbury with the midday Hereford-London express, August 1965
[*G. W. Osborne*

STEAM IN DECLINE

BELOW: No 6998 *Burton Agnes Hall* heads an up empty van train out of the Severn Tunnel near Patchway, July 14, 1964.   This engine was subsequently saved by the Great Western Society and is in course of restoration at Didcot
[*R. C. Riley*